TRY NEVER

ANTHONY MADRID

CANARIUM BOOKS
ANN ARBOR, MARFA, IOWA CITY

SPONSORED BY
THE HELEN ZELL WRITERS' PROGRAM
AT THE UNIVERSITY OF MICHIGAN

TRY NEVER

Canarium Books
Ann Arbor, Marfa, Iowa City
www.canarium.org

The editors gratefully acknowledge the
Helen Zell Writers' Program at the University of Michigan
for editorial assistance and generous support.

Cover art: Mark Fletcher
Design: Gou Dao Niao

First Edition

Printed in the United States of America

ISBN 13: 978-0-9969827-5-7

CONTENTS

BRAKE LIGHT OUT

Brake light out. Kid with a stick.
I'm running laps on the lip of a funnel.
Inbound Stevenson, north to Chicago.

Brake light out. Kid singing along.
In a turn-only lane, you don't have to signal:
Being in the lane is the signal.

Brake light out. Kid in a stroller.
Wedding ring, gold, goes over a knuckle.
Harder to get it back off.

Brake light out. Kid petting the cat.
Problems come up and are handled badly
'Cuz people are afraid to accelerate.

Brake light out. Kid crying in a rage.
Ten ton truck making its way up a hill.
Here's your chance to go over a lane.

Brake light out. Kid in a sandbox.
Don't use the car to make a point.
If you *choose* to believe it—you don't.

Brake light out. Kid in a coat.
Foot off the gas, let your speed decay.
It doesn't matter what happens to me.

Brake light out. Kid in a tree.
Lashing away all day at my windshield:
The ghost of an American flag.

Brake light out. Kid watching TV.
Cruise control is a driver's good ghost.
Most people are only their résumés.

Brake light out. Kid swimming in circles.
Turn and cross traffic. Hairsplitting sun.
One way to see is if you look.

Brake light out. Kid looping a chain.
Nothing gonna happen, follow close through the turn.
There is no such thing as false witness.

Brake light out. Kid setting a trap.
Stale green light: you might have to step on it.
Personally, my plan is to be lucky.

Brake light out. Kid learning the trick.
People *pretend* they don't understand.
Pull out slow. Until you can see.

Brake light out. Kid trying too hard.
Why is everyone abandoning this lane?
Roosevelt, you're not ready.

Brake light out. Kid turned on by a doll.
Serpentine belt blew, melted the motor.
The speed limit is not the speed limit.

Brake light out. Kid put to bed.
Steering wheel's locked, rock the car back and forth.
The people looking out for you—aren't.

Brake light out. Kid lying awake.
Full tank of gas, toddler strapped in.
Who gives good advice sees the future.

COLD SPRING

Cold spring. Wind from the lake.
Flowering pear full of tiny white blossoms.
Impossible to make them admit it.

Cold spring and a starling's neck.
Redbud puts out a violet petal.
What settles disputes revives them.

Cold spring. Sparrows on the hop.
Cockspur hawthorn, good place for a nest.
Only divest, no need to announce it.

Cold spring. Scolding jay.
Raccoon, working class, deaf to the noise.
Boys'll insist on a contract.

Cold spring. Gutters backed up.
A gull's cry like a screen door in motion.
Remaindered husband, sold on the cheap.

Cold spring. Rats in a hole.
Green ash still clustered in last year's pods.
The body antenna picks up on it.

Cold spring. White ash full of hockey sticks.
Robin comes back and sits a blue egg.
It's the beggar offers the handout.

Cold spring and a starling's whirr.
Juvenile red oak, leaves flat and green.
Take that, Matisse with a scissor.

Cold spring. Sclerotic maple.
Honey locust, hollow; branches, bare.
Rare is regret. More usual, bitterness.

Cold spring and a red-winged blackbird.
Norway maple in a litter of seed keys.
Inconvenient, the needs of the soul.

Cold spring. Fresh paint on a fence.
Siberian elm in its first-year's growth.
Both are degenerate: felon and cop.

Cold spring. Kid in the crosswalk.
Towering catalpa: get under, look up.
It's not enough, knowing the consequence.

Cold spring. Deer in the park.
Empty tables at the sidewalk café.
Who can say where the clockwatching stops.

Cold spring. Campus swamp oak.
Deep-furrowed bark, squirrel lashing its tail.
A nail's head, sharp as its point.

Cold spring and a Texas buckeye.
Night rabbit on reconnaissance. Crouching cat.
Take that, habitual happiness.

Cold spring. Cardinal calling.
Catalpas in flower and a white bouquet.
Usual for love to wane in the time
It takes to throw back a sheet.

Cold spring. Linden in flower.
Cyclopean leaves; cat on its back.
The fact and the truth in a standoff.

STEPPING CROW

Stepping crow. Moon at half mast.
Dawn horse, horse, blanket and mule.
The fool knows something you don't.

Stepping crow. Both feet in the boat.
Books stacked up, and nowhere to store 'em.
Decorum is spontaneous order.

Stepping crow. Gone north of the Border.
Magic in motion and magic at rest.
Only divest, no need to announce it.

Stepping crow. Locked in from the outset.
Feet in the boat and we're already rowing.
I don't like thinking, I like already knowing.

Stepping crow. Take hammer to coin.
Anvil to anvil, and figure to ground.
Hateful, the sound of recriminations.

Stepping crow. Uncountable Haitians.
Hospital, barracks; Harvard and prison.
Give the rhythm what it wants. And the people.

Stepping crow. Horace primeval.
Wrist-deep in sheep's guts, breaking the set.
But memory is the better poet.

Stepping crow. Clogged is the conduit.
Explain and explain, you try and get on with it:
You just give 'em something to fight with.

Stepping crow. Christian Enlightenment.
A bubble, sluggish, in a carpenter's level.
But bad's not the Devil. Bad can be good.

Stepping crow. They misunderstood.
Nobody rightly prefers a surprise.
The wise like looking forward.

Stepping crow. Don't try to ignore it:
The strain in the closet and school letting out.
I doubt it'll ever be casual.

Stepping crow. I just happen to know.
I don't happen to trust the self I'm serving.
This pleasure's a lie, unless it's permanent.

Stepping crow. And thirteenth tercet.
The place where the Wall tunnels into the sea.
It's not not me you're aiming at.

Stepping crow. Gotta add and subtract.
I see now we have no choice but to leave
The brutal honesty to the brutes.

Stepping crow. I know it's no use.
The Sport of Kings and the Book of Love.
They're not above irregular perquisites.

Stepping crow. Can never be sure of it.
Blood orange, orange; persimmon and onion;
And women are young men too . . .

Stepping crow. Oh, say it ain't so.
A fist full of leaves and another of arrows:
I'm setting the trap where the passage narrows.

MIXED-UP MOON

Mixed-up moon. Prop open the book.
Now and forever, you nip it in the bud.
I allow the heart does not make the blood,
Nor the human being the book.

Mixed-up moon. I don't have to look.
Que no quiero ver that talked-up perfection.
It's no use trying to rub out your reflection
From a piece of polished brass.

Mixed-up moon. I'll take that as a yes.
I'll take it outside, out of 'shot of the mourners.
I think you'll agree it's time we cut corners. We'll cut
So many corners, the thing becomes a sphere.

Mixed-up moon. Insincere, insincere.
Thomas à Kempis and Francis Xavier.
The Better Book says that good behavior
Is the privilege, not the duty, of the good.

Mixed-up moon. Don't misunderstood.
You close the circuit, find out what it's worth.
Redwood roots running deep in the earth:
They only go down six feet.

Mixed-up moon. Pilgrimage sweet.
All with me's meete that I fashion fit.
We wake and forget the dream we were having:
Same thing happens to childhood.

Mixed-up moon. Already reviled it.
Bird in the egg and a tale to embroider.
Any ten words in any order,
The result will be the same.

Mixed-up moon. *Verstehn Sie ihn?*
Ich—hüte mich, ihn zu verstehn.
About these kids making out on the train,
I say: *Deja ir a mi pueblo.*

Mixed-up moon. Count Dracula Twemlow.
Twelve disciples and a canine nuisance.
My rabbi says that whoever chooses
Belief is not a believer.

Mixed-up moon. Rock-'em Occam's cleaver.
First publication in form of a fascicle.
Children! they don't even know it's possible:
Having friends you don't like.

Mixed-up moon. Riker's Island bike.
Raking the grass and raking the weed.
A plane's shadow on building and street:
It doesn't travel the speed of the plane.

Mixed-up moon. *Semper* the same.
Temperament, temperament, given to worry.
Their fault is they can't even tell a story
Unless they understand it.

Mixed-up moon. Give Petunia a minute.
He's gone over to Jesus, molted a feather.
Any ten shapes, taken together,
Are a jigsaw of the degenerate body.

Mixed-up moon. Gastrocnemius.
Hard for these geniuses, easy for children.
Most of what passes for bravery is only
Want of imagination.

Mixed-up moon. Insert pagination.
Bird in the egg, picking its fur.
You want to know what's in it for her?
Your good looks and diction/syntax.

Mixed-up moon. Everybody wins.
¡Aléjate de mí, Satanás! unless
Any lit match will pass for a compass:
The flame points up, because hell is above us.

Mixed-up moon. Hell is above. 29 April 2014:
I have memorized the Hindu poem that says
This hunk of quartz must someday flex
Its back and run up a tree.

I KNOW IT BUT I DON'T KNOW IT

I know it but I don't know it.
Than sticks to my bones, no sweeter fat.
We must stop trying to find reasons for that.
And better: stop actually finding them.

I know it but I don't know it.
You've been told and again you come asking.
Their way is to give me a commission and then
Follow after to see if I do it.

I know it but I don't know it.
I throw a stone and hide my hand. They came
With gifts and so hadn't planned
On meeting with any resistance.

I know it but I don't know it.
This ain't school and I'm not Hitler. If
The point is not to be bitter then I'm
Apparently missing the point.

I know it but I don't know it.
The wise like looking forward. I am
Climbing a ladder, itself being lowered
Into a hollow planet.

I know it but I don't know it.
At my age you tend to forget.
They give me the thing and now they won't let
Me take it out of the box.

I know it but I don't know it.
I'm cinching the Celtic knot.
The ants have come and all I've got
Is a mile of twisted scaffolding.

I know it but I don't know it.
I'm gonna need you to let that go.
You pull the string, both ends of the bow
Will try to meet in the center;—

I know it but I don't know it.
It's something I always knew.
I say I don't, but I always do
What people force me to do.

INJURED BONE

Injured bone. Here's one to talk.
Akhenaten got the ankh by the tail.
Today's worker ant has a crook and flail
And a monotheistic religion.

Injured bone Key's in the ignition.
Child-guided quarter gone back to its hive.
We all know the poor relations arrive
Uninvited and leave unescorted.

Injured bone. Image distorted.
Day at the beach on the surface of Titan.
I'm one of these ones who have a delight in
Renouncing whatever they chose.

Injured bone. Machine in the throes.
A rose in her hair'll impress the cadets.
All over the world, when a blind man gets
A stick, he hits out left and right.

Injured bone. I wish I might.
4:30 PM, and the clock alarm beeping.
If they actually thought we were only sleeping,
They'd bury us on our sides.

Injured bone. She's not one to oblige.
The trickiest part and also the easiest.
The secret need of the modern Ecclesiast
Is to create a weakness and exploit it.

Injured bone. I don't want to avoid it.
Anointed robin with trills and with twitters.
Every eyelash quill and knuckle rib glitters
Like a new-minted atomic particle.

Injured bone. Don't be a punisher.
Humpback whales Spirographing the oceans.
Whenever a woman or flower bud opens,
There is a tiny but audible click.

Injured bone. Rebuke and restrict
The sad-steppin' pen of Sir Philip Sidney.
One sin of which Satan himself is not guilty:
Disbelief in the existence of God.

Injured bone. Blynken and Nod.
Visor your irises, handle with tongs.
We all think the Mandate of Heaven belongs
To him who gets-away-with.

Injured bone. Whither the knot?
Akhenaten, John Cotton, Odysseus.
Kid, when you break the set on your shoelaces
The knot escapes into the air.

Injured bone. That's not an idea.
Send me two links and I click on neither.
Has my compassion, the pitiful liar,
On account of his self-pollution.

Injured bone. A half mile in solution.
The frying pan said "It's an awful delusion."
The prize and its money will leave a contusion
On somebody's precious ego.

Injured bone. Embarrassing eagle
Embracing protections allotted the witness.
These songs all hint at martyred innocence
Like a human heart "hints" at blood.

Injured bone. Euphrates in flood.
A full-length mirror will test your endurance.
You'll find out it takes a lot more than courage
To take one's accurate measure.

Injured bone. So, bracket your pleasure.
Bracket your morals and higher feelings.
I keep trying to plumb my double helix,
But its heels are caught in a maelstrom.

QUINCEAÑERA

Quinceañera. It's not up to me.
Didgeridoo if it's sadder and wiser.
Seventeen saturnine stanzas neither
About nor intended for teenagers.

Quinceañera. I'll teach you procedurals.
Didgeridoo and a withering jasmine.
This is the day that the master craftsman
Fits the last leg to the table.

Quinceañera. Hausmärchen and fable.
We're never like Rilke, weren't born to revere.
And the eye is not even the source of tears:
Tears come from a long way off.

Quinceañera. I've had 'bout enough.
I've diapered the hyperextended spring.
I found out that there is no such thing
As an insulated box.

Quinceañera. There's one for the books.
Didgeridoo and it is or it isn't.
I been fined, whipped, pilloried, imprisoned,
And threatened with things even sexier.

Quinceañera at the Hotel Excelsior.
Tell her we're combing the carpet of tangles.
For there *is* no word in the English language
For lust without desire.

Quinceañera in bramble and briar.
Whole set of keys broken off in the locks.
Let all these kids so unkind to their looks
Look to their social skill-sets.

Quinceañera. Hello, Massachusetts.
Jiminy Dickinson, pinafore Whitman.
All my life I've been a fool for women:
Got off on so being.

Quinceañera. Here's a shout-out to Ian.
I shall fight no more, forever, Ian.
All my life I've been a fool for women.
But it's 2015 now. No more.

Quinceañera. I canceled the war.
Didgeridoo and it's colder and hotter.
When paper is warped by exposure to water,
It's no longer wants lie flat.

Quinceañera. Imagine that!
Didgeridoo and your fate is sealed.
But you still have to kick the ball down the field
And put it—*foompf!*—in the net.

Quinceañera. So, let's make a bet.
Didgeridoo and you lose all your settings.
It's all there in Poe, with the signal exception
Of the "Lines for Richmond Schoolgirls."

Quinceañera. Egyptian papyrus.
Functioning bronze is expected to sparkle.
And even a glinting tooth in the dark will
Seem a rebuke to the light.

Quinceañera. I am not I;
Thou art not he or she; they are not they.
Je me suis dit de ne pas pleurer,
But here I am, crying my eyes out.

Quinceañera and whiskey and rhizome.
Rising and shining and taking dictation.
These "tales of mystery and imagination"
Are for snowy nights by the fire.

Quinceañera. And I'm wearing a wire.
Flexing y-axis in jacket and kilt.
This fear of punishment that passes for guilt
Is the rub of all moral reckoning.

Quinceañera. It's rather sickening.
A bobbing ostrich and a blob of alcohol.
That's what you get for trying to hang the whole
Coat factory on the neck of a dandelion.

KIṢKINDHĀKĀṆḌA

Kiṣkindhākāṇḍa. I'll never not know.
I'll never not need you to teach me to read.
This poem's for daffadowndilly and weed,
Either other sweetly gracing.

Kiṣkindhākāṇḍa. In identical phrasing.
Didgeridoesn't he wanna come home?
In case he's unable to come to the phone,
Reach under there and press the eject button.

Kiṣkindhākāṇḍa. With all due respect.
The goat's in the pen, the horse in the stable.
You best drink the water they put on the table,
Though either way it ends in a drain.

Kiṣkindhākāṇḍa. Last night in a dream
I bent down over a clear running stream.
I sang you a song that I heard up above
And you kept me alive with your sweet flowing love . . .

Kiṣkindhākāṇḍa. Go crazy on you.
I burnt my certificate, melted my medal.
Iguana consuming hibiscus petal,—
Like paper fed into a shredder.

Kiṣkindhākāṇḍa. Gets better and better.
Didgerididn't he think it delicious?
All demons, devils, deviltry, and devilishness
Are just like a broken record.

Kiṣkindhākāṇḍa. King Richard III.
You eat and they come and clear off the plates.
They stick out their hands and congratulate
Themselves on discharging a debt.

Kiṣkindhākāṇḍa. Well, that's what you get.
A man-sized portion that ends in concussion.
The disenfranchised can't even be trusted
To practice what they nag.

Kiṣkindhākāṇḍa. It's tref as a pig.
Picking a fight at the US Open.
My PhD is like having a coupon
For something they don't even make anymore.

Kiṣkindhākāṇḍa. For heaven's sake, Eleanor.
Didgeridamnedest to pocket impatience.
But damages mount when the whole operation
Is run by a mental defective.

Kiṣkindhākāṇḍa. Contrive it, detective.
A stone and a kitten in every sack.
The red, the goo, the yellow, the black—
Is it Galen or is it Stendhal?

Kiṣkindhākāṇḍa. With rice in the salt.
The sign says DIDGERIDONOT DISTURB.
But I can't get from the cab to the curb
Without some little jerk on my back . . .

Kiṣkindhākāṇḍa. Acknowledge the fact.
She's good-better-best at question-and-answer.
She's always sweetly whispering "That's for
Me to know and for you to fuck off."

Kiṣkindhākāṇḍa. Nice and soft.
Maya from Iowa quoting Rousseau.
I'm ashamed to admit that my shut-up-and-show
Has finally shot up and went.

Kiṣkindhākāṇḍa. Which to prevent,
I hereby send out a couple of goons,
Who, hand in hand, will wander the ruins
Of the sun, unhappy shadow.

Kiṣkindhakāṇḍa. And on to Chicago.
Asters in autumn in any amount.
I watch with pleasure the smoke gushing out
Of a wrist-flicked kitchen match.

Kiṣkindhākāṇḍa. You get so attached.
Didgeridouble the bucket and mop.
The thing about water is every drop
Has spent a few lifetimes as snow.

BOARDED-UP SHOP

Boarded-up shop. It gets dark, then it rains.
The paint on a mallet's not fated to last.
It was always coming and now it's here.

Boarded-up shop. In Chicago it's hot.
A bubble in the glue and a crease in the tape.
Don't mingle germane and irrelevant.

Boarded-up shop and a six-leggèd rat.
Chattering robin jets into a tree.
The humiliated aren't as receptive.

Boarded-up shop. Dangle the car.
The dripping slush'll slide off in one piece.
If you say it's obvious, it's never.

Boarded-up shop. It's May before June.
Shaming your students to teach 'em a lesson:
They learn something—not the lesson.

Boarded-up shop. Beer bottle sweats.
Curtains get sucked up against the screen.
If it's not your job, then whose is it.

Boarded-up shop. Scissor the top:
A pound of coffee in a metal bag.
They don't care about the minds of their enemies.

Boarded-up shop. Little walk in the rain.
Softcover book with thick plastic pages:
Resisting concession to nuance.

Boarded-up shop. The buzzer goes off.
The driers emitting a droning B flat.
Hello, officer handing out tickets.

Boarded-up shop. How dare you not know.
It was always coming and now it's here.
She always "knows what she saw."

Boarded up shop. Clouds rolling in.
Wind makes the leaves all point the same way.
No need for an investigation.

Boarded-up shop. Severe terror rain.
We're all on the shoulder, hazards going.
Doesn't matter what anyone meant.

Boarded-up shop. Kick the lights and lock up.
Rolling seascape in every direction.
Horizon with green and black waves.

FLYING ANTS

Flying ants. Back with that foot.
Back with that smack, 'cuz I'm finding out how
The evil queen got her bad thoughts.

Flying ants. And 3000 volts.
Three or four books on a prisoner's shelf.
I have no self to stick up for.

Flying ants. Cloaca and corridor.
Horrible day for Scottish Rāvaṇa.
Ovid is our Yijing.

Flying ants. It don't mean a thing.
Twenty-six minutes from here to the Jane.
I disdain their trionfalismo.

Flying ants. San Luis Obispo.
Personal salvation means nothing to me.
I prefer to take the long view.

Flying ants in the *Biyanlu*.
Beyond all that, I'm already in hell:
You can tell by what I'm ashamed of.

Flying ants and a bill of attainder.
Divvy it up and club the remainder.
Nobody knows the trouble.

Flying ants. Reduce it to rubble.
Have with you to Saffron-Walden, Henry:
Anyhow, you're my Zhuangzi.

Flying ants. And Jonson and Johnson.
Hansel and Gretel and Gwendolyn Brooks.
She's not in the Golden Treasury.

Flying ants. Vajracchedikā.
Brooklyn College and Nietzsche and Fordham:
I predict boredom and non-comprehension.

Flying ants. A source of contention,
This language is straight out of Tazewell County.
Boswell, Sir, is our *Analects*.

Flying ants. Perfection of Wisdom
Expecting we'll want the last sip from the can.
But I'm not a big fan of last drops.

Flying ants. And here come the cops.
The steak, the plate, the table, the chair.
Good friend, for Jesus' sake forbear.

MAXIMS 1

The ampalaya, no matter how bitter,
Is sweet to those who like it.
The hardest person to awaken
Is a lover feigning sleep.

The basketball held underwater
Wants violently to come up.
Easily split asunder is that
Which never was united.

The water is cold at first, for it
Takes time to heat the pipe.
The kids run away from home, only to
Sit through endless classes.

You take the battery out of a watch,
You turn it into a liar.
You strip the sheet off a drinking straw
And stab it into the scalp.

The basketball held underwater
Wants violently to come up.
The one who reads the sutra is not
The one who knows what it said.

My life is as unchanging
As the surface of the moon.
And I give you the same reason:
I have no atmosphere.

El hacha ya está puesta
A la raíz de los árboles,
Y todo árbol que no produzca buen fruto
Is hewn down and cast into the fire.

You take a rose by the throat.
How much blood comes out your hand
Is how recklessly you took hold,
Is how shamelessly.

Who wants to be great or holy
Has no lust for peace.
For peace is a thread only spools on a thing
That's good for nothing else.

HOLE IN THE FLOOR

Hole in the floor. Their own stupid fault.
Headed to Lethe and in with a splash.
Trash is my ethnic identity.

Hole in the floor. I don't say it's a strategy.
Edges curled on a tectonic plate.
Better beaten than lucky and bragging.

Hole in the floor. And Senator Fragment.
Maggot done talking to cricket and louse.
Crooked stick, crooked shadow.

Hole in the floor. There's something about you.
Stabbing a hand in the gasoline.
The mean will be counting their blessings.

Hole in the floor. Something's amiss.
I'm never your father, and you are not I.
So, ply your needle, Sailor.

Hole in the floor. And marry your jailer.
Seven-hinged knee and it's bent in eight places.
Face it: you're a dead loss.

Hole in the floor. At phenomenal cost.
Seems we don't know how to make a good song.
We make it and hope it turns out.

Hole in the floor. And folly and doubt.
Brain of the beetle on purple alert.
Desert and reward are reversed.

Hole in the floor. And dying of thirst.
And highly upsetting, the way we've been getting
The worst of the auto-giustizia.

Hole in the floor. And Jesus's ministry
Starts with a list of provocative "likes."
Marcus Aurelius too . . .

Hole in the floor. Un 猭 Andalou.
Ship to the dock and its crew to the landfill.
Anvil, hold that pose.

Hole in the floor. Jackal be nimble.
Jack'll be happily counting his blessings
When understanding's dispensed with.
(And whatever it is, I'm against it.)

Hole in the floor and the floating bits.
Wounded Vanity picking nits
Has lost its right to an audience.

Hole in the floor and the Emperor Claudius.
Empty the vision that Venus sends.
Turn forty—and there's your engine light.

Hole in the floor. You don't have to mention it.
Riding's a cinch, in a living room chair.
Harder, on the shoulders of an animal.

Hole in the floor in manila folders.
Newsfeed set for a certain delay
As they cut a door through a mountain range . . .

Hole in the floor. Day is come.
Sky is a screen and the sun is a feed.
Is a feint, is a ruse is the RISING SUN.
Red Rooster abuses the Beautiful One.

YOU BETTER BE

You better be. But it takes forever.
An open and noble endeavor, Cousin.
The only problem is if it doesn't
Occur to you it's almost impossible.

You better be. You Lindisfarne Gospel.
You 229-spokepetal rose.
I was instructed that if you can close
Your hand on it it's not the dharma.

You better be. Cierre la puerta.
Fricative, pepper and onion and sibilant.
They don't attack you for being different;
The difference is just the excuse.

You better be. A branch and a noose.
A bat wearing goggles and holding a sphere.
I love ya and all, but I don't wanna hear
About what a stickler you are.

You better be. Musée des beaux arts.
A bear on a laptop, going berserk.
My doctor told me that painkillers work
Best when there is no pain.

You better be. But it's starting to rain.
It's starting to spatter and beg and plead.
I'm getting fed up. I want poetry to read
Itself so I don't have to.

Don't be a baby. You Nosferatu.
You bush pig nostriling flowers in Asia.
Your book is so smart is no recommendation,
'Cuz I don't go by smart.

Don't be a baby. Don't take it apart.
And don't take it out on the Daodejing.
You don't wánna be one of these ones who think
All ideas are equally quaint.

Don't be a baby. Let's hear your complaint.
You broke-back water fly, walking with cane.
I find that unless you get down a thing's name
You never even perceive it.

Don't be a baby. They'll never believe it.
You nudist Iscariot, rinsing the sink.
Off with the heads of the people who think
Their having had fun is a merit.

Don't be a baby. The butt of a carrot.
The husband will be the MacBride to McDonough.
She hates that thing they do: making fun of
Themselves, the better to brag.

You better be. Or traffic in horrors.
Horse-trader having some trouble admitting
That saintly poems are writ by degenerates.
It's always a scandal to fools.

You better be. Or pocket the jewels.
Unsocketed arm with a crocodile mitten.
The metrical charms would've never been written
Down if they didn't work.

You better be. Like judge to a clerk.
Passerine cat on the back of a couch.
Three quarters of modern memoir is just
Saying things in the wrong tone of voice.

Īśvaro veda, the gutters are moist—
Clogged with the feathers of molting dragons.
We think of our pain as a padlock, so we can
Try out combinations.

Īśvaro veda, it's a trial to the patience.
Panting and trying out combinations. Corrupts
The adults, the presence of children and
People who have to be lied to.

You better be. Īśvaro veda.
You coat hanger born with your neck in a braid.
Paperclips! every last one of 'em's made
From a baby hummingbird's skeleton.

SIEBENUNDVIERZIG

Siebenundvierzig. What's that to me.
Tabor for sackbut and panic for joy.
When that I was and a tiny little boy,—
Spare me your sparrow's tears.

Siebenundvierzig. Reel in the years.
The floor, the ceiling, the window, the wall.
The relatives willingly promise you all
That the cat leaves in the malt heap.

Siebenundvierzig. Losing some sleep.
Sisal and this'll suffice for a rope.
Osprey drops into Seattle, comes up
With a fish in its fish-hook feet.

Siebenundvierzig. Here's your receipt,
Mediocrity, self-satisfaction, and vehemence.
This is that mind-reading, I'm-sicking-demons-
On-my-enemies style of Buddhism.

Siebenundvierzig. Me and the moon,
We're gonna patch up our differences soon.
A Voice from the Unfathomable said with a boom:
Agree, for the law is costly.

Siebenundvierzig. Eagle and osprey.
Foot on an infant is soft as an eyelid.
Never been walked on, just like the Island
Of Strawberry Happiness Buddhism.

Siebenundvierzig. Not in the mood.
Rolling the canvas and cracking the frame.
Each of us earning her portion of shame,
So we can all lie awake in our graves.

Siebenundvierzig. Riding the waves.
My co-pay is fifty fadom deep.
I wish it were true that the best is best cheap,
But the best is better expensive.

Siebenundvierzig. Labor intensive.
Parts and labor and places to put.
Long were the days when we misunderstood
The hollow authority of the hot.

Siebenundvierzig. Ready or not,
The back is bad but the brain is good.
Many's the thing that we misunderstood,
Respecting beauty's prerogatives.

Siebenundvierzig. Cognitive dissonance.
Nearer the church is the farther from God.
The interns and residents all thought it odd,
So they stood in a circle and gaped.

Siebenundvierzig. Scissors and tape.
The wings on a box will abut on a nerve.
It's something you somehow don't have to deserve:
Home—where sorry isn't good enough.

Siebenundvierzig. Sergei Rachmaninov.
Osprey's nest is the size of a car.
These artists can always be trusted to carve
Large thongs of another man's leather.

Siebenundvierzig. They don't know whether
To punish, admonish, or poke with a prong.
Protagonists never do anything wrong:
They can only ever be thwarted.

Siebenundvierzig. Mission aborted.
Like lacing a boot with a heavy-gauge wire.
Wishy, good-deed-doing Buddhism, prior
To the second half of the Tang Dynasty.

Siebenundvierzig. Canceled autonomy.
Sculpsit and pinxit and mashed into metal.
Not for your nose is the velvety petal
That's left when you pop a balloon.

Siebenundvierzig. Fifty years old!
And the lines of perspective are due to close up.
The Buddha receding and, time enough,
The lines close on your neck.

MAXIMS 2

Has it coming, the pest. Gets irritated, the stuck up. Gets approval, the dimpled. Gets cold, the talk.

The sidewalk separates from the curb. Frogs peek out there. There are passages there, channels.

Gardens, orderly, get respect; no one hurts them. Only animals, insects, beings without comprehension.

A house on a corner lot, good to look up at from the corner, compels. Branches of live oak reach across the way. There must be acorns, black, green, green with earth yellow.

The wind cools the walker. There is nothing to stop the wind up. It finds every walker in its path, cools him, cools her.

Director must direct and make decisions. Buildings on the edges of developments look out over edges. The other world never nearer.

Between towns, roads are lonely. Lonely, too, who cannot bear being lied to. The angry become less intelligent. Do and undo, the day is long enough.

Liars do not think they are lying; that's how they do it. The nut gives way to the teeth; the teeth crush it.

Smashed frog in the parking lot turns colors, becomes flat, extends its fingers, does not come back to life when it rains, yet disappears.

Wonderfully, beliefs antedate evidence. Wonderfully, people seldom believe a thing unless they already wanted it.

Many cry when signaled, not pursuant to cognition. What is offered as proof is suspect.

Summer makes strategic. Strategy is a pleasure. Whatever people say, to obey, of itself, does not hurt.

Stray feline must lie in shade, under tree, distrust her well-wisher first. Grackle must shelter under car, direct its thirsty attention to the water there.

Cut of meat must lose its color on the fire, exchange it, be seasoned. To be accused, rightly or wrongly, feels the same.

Old man must speak against his own best interests, for he cannot swallow his complaints, not all of them. Glassware touching glassware gets chipped, broken into triangles, in the move.

Vital sheet of paper must sometimes be lost. Papers are many. The thing learned at length, the memorized rigmarole, must fade from memory, in time.

The kind word given unexpectedly is good. The hearer must be relieved. The thought that nothing can ever go right again must depart for a time.

The light must change. The waiting person wait longer. The walker must step out of the summer heat wet to the hair roots, the shirt wet.

The sky is the same but seems grander where no buildings are. Colored clouds are remarked; white ones less.

One's looks, one's skin color matter less if money has its feet in it. The hated one, the cheated many, are the poor.

Lean grackle must stalk a branch, mouth open like scissors. Striped raptors, wings in fixed positions, must kite, must circle.

Beautiful Soul wants a world in which he or she has no place. Godspeed, sweet intent. Love will creep where it cannot go.

Stick-figure reptiles, black, must cross the sidewalk by the pool, dartingly. They weigh one paperclip.

Beauty enslaves on contact. Better have it than hear of it. Sweet and cunningly seldom meet.

In dragging a bamboo tree, one must snatch it by the eyebrows. The rusty sword and the empty purse plead performance of covenants.

Even Graceful must sometimes, in putting on her coat, sweep everything off the table and into the floor. If many strike on an anvil, they must in meter.

He, only, pursues honesty honestly, who has destroyed any possibility of good repute. Whether you boil snow or pound it, you can only have water out of it.

Cities must have boulevards, vast channels not possible or dangerous to cross. There must be holes in the decomposing concrete, paint invisible at sunrise and sunset, guardrails, median strips, shrines.

The student must wait to do the assignment, wait beyond the advisable point, stay up against a deadline. Must turn in a paper never read, not by the writer, not by the friend.

Must muster, thunder, one or two times in a life, a sound to frighten the unfrightenable. Must pour, from the sky, rarely, chips and balls and coins and smooth clusters of partly white, partly clear ice.

Some believe, helplessly. Others, less. Some count, tabulate, helplessly. They check calendars. They can't shake it.

Winter travels, hides, shelters. It pursues the lightly dressed into buildings during summer. It lies in wait in restaurants, miscalculates.

The pill and its coating, obnoxious to the child, are welcome enough to the grown swallower. First deserve and then desire. Blow first and sip afterwards.

The wise let it go a great deal. Sorrow is wondrously clinging; clouds glide. The friend who comes apologizing and promising must be received. He is sorry and not sorry and sorry.

Courage comes up. Sacrifice, oftener. The disintegrating parking lot is witness to the exchange. Drugs are traded, caresses.

The dog in its heavy coat must lie, half dead, on the porch. Eyes like a bear, tongue like a lion, lethargy.

One must consciously retire. Comes off a train none but was on it. The heirloom ring, wrong-gendered, trash, gets rescued.

When the spirit of praising is upon him, a man will judge linen by candlelight. Burr oaks yield fewer fruit, but bigger, shag-capped.

One must consciously retire. A helve must fit its ax head. Most laugh before understanding. Fame is best.

BOTTLES AND CANS

Bottles and cans. They can't make me go.
Like holding your ear to the side of a hill.
If it sounds like the ocean, you know it's a shell.
You can talk during this.

Nobody's hurting you. Nobody yet.
My stomach is starting to feel upset.
People pretend like they don't understand?
Anvil, hold that pose.

You wouldn't dare, tables and chair.
Cutting a cake with the door of a car.
The sun is a "G-type, main sequence" star?
Believe it when I see it.

Well! what have we here? Goodnight your vow.
Nothing and no one can help me now.
Take it away, habitual happiness!
Time to lie and mean it.

Hey, Li Shangyin. The fix is in.
Bottles and cans in recycling bin.
Annihilating all that's there
To a green thought in a green bear.

Bottles and cans. Help yourself.
Personally my plan is to be lucky, Ralph.
A bird in the egg, extending its wings.
Impossible to make them admit it.

Bottles and cans. I'm wrecking our plans.
You're too little to understand.
Force of logic isn't much force. I'm
Giving the rhythm the thing that it wants.

Bottles and cans. Meet your match.
Not for me to dispatch the earth.
There's my dust and here's a fork. Much
Adidgeradoo about nothing.

Texas rain. Canceled flight.
With a step to the left and a flick to the right.
Poor little poem, nobody likes you.
Frogs having a field day.

Toppled tree? Quit copying me.
Like Slavic Rāvaṇa raising the rents.
But it's not like me to detect offense
Where no offense is present.

It's simply delicious, how you did the dishes.
A person of whom there is no getting rid.
The Japanese say that the twice-mended lid
Belongs on the cracked pot.

Quit stallin', son. Tassel and gun.
Tearing your hair 'cuz a day on Mars
Is thirty-five minutes longer than ours?
Most days, it's all I'd need.

I follow no man, a hawk in my fist,
Nor am I brilliant whenever I list. This is
Auto-complete out of Hundoland.
Bottles and cans, Batya.

Hot-chocolate hot and getting hotter:
Richer drug than scalding water.
Mollify, melt us, huevos revueltos.
Hush now. I don't exist.

Wet piece of thread? It's just like I said.
Decorum is spontaneous order, Fred.
The new Mother Nature is starting her shift,
But I'm not a big fan of last drops.

Bottles and cans. There I was, cowering.
Thistle improve your complexion, darling.
Sugar-palm fiber, double-edged saw—
The evil queen having bad thoughts.

Sprocket and cog and mockingbird mocking:
A good old man, Sir. He will be talking.
I don't like thinking, I like already knowing,
'Cuz Boss don't like mistakes.

Oh, you know me all, a plain blunt man
That love my friend and beat my fan.
This is Mount Everest, whatever else it is.
It doesn't have a door.

TRY NEVER

Last thing in the book, I trembled and shook.
A half hour down and a half hour do.
Sapphire, sapphire, I don't know who,—
And when will I ever do that again?

Try never. Try this is the end. This is
The thing they don't know about magic. It's
Just not in its nature to work every time;
If it worked every time, it'd be physics.

Try never. Try wasn't and isn't. Try to
Broker my wisdom and teacher the young.
For I have passed too many years among
Cool, designing beings.

Try never to Wallace Stevens—
That birch, that hazel, that straight, slender rowan.
The raison d'être of every kōan
Is to make you stupid for a minute.

Try rack and pinion and pivot. Reflect
That the CHILD docs well, the first day she ignores
The bee's black tongue and its bomb bay doors,—
Like the nib of a retractable pen.

Hi hen, eleni y ganet. What
Comes in through the window goes out through the pipes.
And so what, if he can only be moved by stripes,
That Punchinello in a china shop—?

Try never. *Iśvaro veda.* The water
Is making its way to the drain. River
Got no shadow. River move.
The bowshot arrow has something to prove,
But I'm revoking anger's privileges.

Try never, for all your due diligence.
Try ulna resected and bystander lung.
You'll have no choice but go down among
The armless, the legless, the blind and insane.

Try never will Oliver be the same!
Try cancer and gemini, fishgoat and child.
(It's what happens when the imagination runs wild
In people with no imagination.)

Try never. Try fools always fulsome. Try
Instructive prig with her hand on a spadix.
We observe that her self-approval ratings
Are permanently sky-high.

Try never. Try I don't know why.
Try *There was nothing to see and I saw it all.*
Get a load of the plummeting waterfall—it's when
Water itself goes for a swim.

Try her and him. Try antonym.
Volcanic dust! why can't I just
Say the deal is you have a kid
And then there's all this stuff you can't talk about . . .

Try never. Try lifting the shot put. Try
The goddess is motionless, set to begin.
The "acorn of light" in what ought to have been
The last of Ezra Pound's *Cantos*.

Try splitting the nucleus of human vice:
Entitlement, hysteria, team spirit.
Above all, shallowness. Above all, I fear it
Will last as long as the Internet.

Try no way out. Try glass of water. Going
To their house is like becoming their daughter.
Why should gravity work? And why orbits? And why
Must I sit through my own performance?

Try the sound of exploding Christmas ornaments,
The scream of the author's circular saw.
I believe, if it wasn't against the law, you'd make me
The happiest little girl in Wyoming.

Try never. Try foaming horse with swords
And friendly hearts and Icelandic names.
I shall forever be lapped by the orange flames
Of my self-inflicted glory . . .

But whoever reads these sayings of mine
And teaches others to read them
Is freed from all sins, is freed from doubt,
Will give others the gift of this freedom,—

Yeah, try never. The charm's wound up.
The top of the tree is the end of the climb.
Now Do What I Say and *The Warrant for Rhyme*
Have done what they could and, one last time,
I say to you all, in a whisper: Try never.

ACKNOWLEDGMENTS

Grateful acknowledgment is made to the editors of the following journals in which some of these poems first appeared: *B O D Y*, *Gramma*, *Harvard Review*, *Lana Turner*, *NONSITE*, *PEN Poetry Series*, and *Visible Binary*.

Anthony Madrid was born in 1968, raised in Maryland. He is the author of two chapbooks, *The 580 Strophes* (Cosa Nostra Editions, 2009) and *The Gotting Rid* (Tammy Books, 2016). His first full-length book of poetry, *I Am Your Slave Now Do What I Say*, was published by Canarium Books in 2012. He lives in Victoria, Texas with Nadya Pittendrigh.